# How to Become a Social Media Manager with no experience

## Your Roadmap to Social Media Management

By

M.I.Fazil

# Table of contents

# Introduction

The social media landscape is a dynamic force, shaping how we connect, consume information, and make purchasing decisions. For businesses of all sizes, it presents a powerful opportunity to reach new audiences, build brand awareness, and achieve marketing goals. But navigating this ever-evolving space requires a strategic approach and the right skill set.

Are you ready to transform your social media presence from good to great?

Our comprehensive Social Media Manager Guide equips you with the knowledge and tools to become a social media master. Whether you're a marketing enthusiast, a budding entrepreneur, or looking to enhance your existing skillset, this book empowers you to:

• Develop Winning Social Media Strategies: Learn to define clear goals, identify your target audience, and craft a data-driven plan for success.
• Master Engaging Content Creation: Discover the secrets to creating compelling content that resonates with your audience across different platforms.
• Become a Scheduling and Publishing Pro: Unleash the power of scheduling tools and optimize your posting strategy for maximum reach.

• Unlock the Secrets of Social Media Analytics: Learn to analyze data, measure progress, and refine your approach based on valuable insights.

• Foster Thriving Communities:  Develop the skills to manage online communities, respond to comments and messages, and build genuine brand loyalty.

• Stay Ahead of the Curve:  Gain the knowledge to stay informed about the latest social media trends and algorithm changes.

This trail is your passport to social media mastery.  Are you ready to dive in and unlock the power of social media? Let's get started!

Social media has become an essential marketing tool for businesses of all sizes. A well-managed social media presence can help you:

• Increase brand awareness: Reach a wider audience and establish your brand as a thought leader in your industry.

• Drive engagement: Build relationships with your customers and foster a loyal community.

• Generate leads and sales: Convert followers into paying customers through targeted campaigns and promotions.

• Gain valuable insights: Learn about your audience's preferences and tailor your marketing strategy accordingly.

A social media manager orbit can equip you with the skills and knowledge you need to achieve these goals. By taking a way, you'll learn how to:

• Develop a winning social media strategy
• Create engaging content for different platforms
• Schedule and publish posts effectively
• Analyze social media data and track your progress
• Manage social media communities and respond to comments and messages
• Stay up-to-date with the latest social media trends and algorithms

# Chapter_1

## Welcome to the Social Media Marketing Landscape: Your Guide to Social Media Management

Social media has transformed from a place to connect with friends and family into a powerful marketing tool. In today's digital age, businesses of all sizes are leveraging social media platforms to reach new audiences, build brand awareness, and drive sales. This course, Social Media Manager, equips you with the foundational knowledge and practical skills to become a leader in this dynamic field.

This first chapter, "Introduction to Social Media Marketing," lays the groundwork for your journey as a social media manager. We'll explore the core concepts of social media marketing, understand its role within the digital marketing landscape, and unveil the exciting opportunities it presents.

### Unveiling the Power of Social Media Marketing

Social media marketing involves utilizing social media platforms to achieve specific marketing goals for your business. Think of it as a conversation happening in a virtual town square – a place to engage with potential and existing customers, share valuable content, and build brand loyalty. But unlike traditional marketing methods, social media fosters a two-way communication channel, allowing you to listen, respond, and build meaningful relationships with your audience.

Here are some of the key benefits of incorporating social media marketing into your strategy:

• Increased Brand Awareness: Expand your reach and introduce your brand to a wider audience. Social media allows you to tap into a vast network of users, putting your brand in front of potential customers who might not have found you otherwise.

• Enhanced Brand Engagement: Social media provides a platform for direct interaction with your audience. Respond to comments, answer questions, and participate in conversations – all in real-time. This fosters a sense of community and builds stronger connections with your customers.

• Lead Generation and Sales Growth: Convert your social media followers into paying customers. By sharing valuable content and targeted promotions, you can nurture leads and guide them through the sales funnel.

• Valuable Customer Insights: Gain a deeper understanding of your target audience. Social media listening tools allow you to analyze conversations, identify trends, and glean valuable insights into your audience's preferences and needs.

• Cost-Effective Marketing: Social media offers a relatively inexpensive way to reach a large audience. While paid advertising options exist, organic content creation and community management can be highly effective without a significant financial investment.

**Understanding the Digital Marketing Ecosystem**

Social media marketing doesn't exist in isolation. It's an integral part of a broader digital marketing strategy. Let's explore how social media interacts with other digital marketing channels:

• Search Engine Optimization (SEO): Social media can play a role in improving your website's search ranking. By sharing content and building backlinks from social media platforms, you can signal to search engines that your content is valuable and relevant.

• Content Marketing: Social media is a fantastic platform for distributing your content – blog posts, infographics, videos – and reaching a wider audience.

• Email Marketing: Social media can be used to grow your email list. Encourage your followers to subscribe to your email newsletter for exclusive content and promotions.

• Paid Advertising: Leverage paid advertising options on social media platforms to target specific demographics and interests, maximizing the reach and impact of your campaigns.

By working in conjunction with other digital marketing channels, social media creates a cohesive and powerful marketing strategy.

**The Road Ahead: Your Social Media Management Journey**

This trail equips you with the skills and knowledge to navigate the exciting world of social media marketing. In the coming chapters, we'll delve deeper into:

• Developing a Winning Social Media Strategy: Learn how to define your target audience, set SMART goals, and craft a strategy to achieve them.
• Crafting Compelling Content: Discover the secrets to creating engaging content (text, images, video) that resonates with your audience on different platforms.
• Mastering the Social Media Landscape: Uncover the unique features and functionalities of major platforms like Facebook, Instagram, Twitter, and more.
• Building and Managing Online Communities: Learn how to foster brand loyalty by building thriving online communities and responding effectively to comments and messages.
• Data, Analytics, and Reporting: Discover how to track your social media performance, measure

campaign success, and make data-driven decisions.

• Staying Ahead of the Curve:  Explore emerging social media trends and adapt your strategy for the ever-evolving digital landscape.

By the end of this itinerary, you'll be well-equipped to launch successful social media campaigns, manage online communities, and become a valuable asset in the world of digital marketing.  So, buckle up and get ready to dive into the exciting world of social media marketing!

.

# Chapter-2

## Building a Winning Social Media Strategy: The Roadmap to Success

In the last chapter, we explored the power of social media marketing and its role in the digital landscape. Now, it's time to translate that knowledge into action. This chapter, "Building a Social Media Strategy," equips you with the essential framework to develop a winning social media strategy that delivers real results.

Think of a social media strategy as your roadmap to success. It defines your destination (goals), outlines the route you'll take (tactics), and equips you with the tools you need to navigate the journey (resources and budget). Here's a step-by-step approach to crafting a social media strategy that will propel your brand forward:

### Step 1: Know Your Audience – Target Like a Pro

Before diving headfirst into content creation, take a step back and identify your target audience. Who are you trying to reach with your social media efforts? Understanding their demographics, interests, online behavior, and pain points is crucial for crafting content that resonates.

Here are some methods to gain a deeper understanding of your target audience:

• Market research: Analyze existing customer data, conduct surveys, or leverage social listening tools to understand audience preferences and online conversations.
• Buyer personas: Develop detailed buyer personas that represent your ideal customers, outlining their demographics, goals, and challenges.

By creating a clear picture of your target audience, you can tailor your social media strategy to speak directly to their needs and interests.

## Step 2: Setting SMART Goals – Measurable Milestones

Now that you know who you're targeting, it's time to define what success means for your social media efforts. Setting clear, measurable goals (SMART goals) provides direction and allows you to track progress along the way.

Here are the key elements of a SMART goal:

• Specific: Clearly define what you want to achieve. Do you want to increase brand awareness, generate leads, or boost website traffic?

• Measurable: Quantify your goals with metrics you can track, such as follower growth, engagement rate, or website clicks.

• Attainable: Set ambitious yet achievable goals to ensure motivation and progress.

• Relevant: Align your goals with your overall marketing objectives and business strategy.

• Time-bound: Establish a timeframe for achieving your goals to maintain focus and accountability.

Examples of SMART goals for social media include:

• Increase brand awareness by 20% within 3 months, as measured by follower growth on key platforms.

• Generate 50 qualified leads per month through targeted social media campaigns.

• Drive 10% more website traffic from social media channels in the next quarter.

**Step 3: Choosing the Right Platforms – Where Your Audience Lives**

With your target audience and goals defined, it's time to select the social media platforms where they spend their time. Don't spread yourself too thin! Focus on the platforms where you can reach a significant portion of your target audience and tailor your content accordingly.

Here's a quick overview of some popular social media platforms and their strengths:

• Facebook: A broad reach platform ideal for brand awareness, community building, and targeted advertising.
• Instagram: A visually-driven platform perfect for showcasing products, sharing lifestyle content, and engaging with influencers.
• Twitter: A real-time platform great for news updates, customer service, and thought leadership content.
• LinkedIn: A professional networking platform ideal for B2B marketing, employer branding, and content marketing.

By understanding the strengths of each platform and aligning them with your target audience and goals, you can make informed decisions about where to invest your resources.

## Step 4: Content is King – Crafting Compelling Stories

Now comes the fun part - content creation! Engaging content is the heart and soul of any successful social media strategy. Here are some tips for crafting compelling content that resonates with your audience:

• Know your content pillars: Define core themes and topics relevant to your brand and audience interests.

• Variety is key: Mix up content formats (text, images, videos) to keep your audience engaged.

• Focus on value: Provide valuable information, entertainment, or inspiration to your audience.

• Storytelling matters: Weave narratives into your content to connect with your audience on an emotional level.

• Maintain brand consistency: Ensure your content aligns with your brand voice and visual identity.

By consistently creating high-quality content that adds value to your audience's lives, you'll establish yourself as a thought leader and attract a loyal following.

# Chapter-3

## Social Media Content Marketing: The Art of Engaging Your Audience

In the previous chapters, we explored the importance of crafting a winning social media strategy and identifying your target audience. Now, it's time to turn your strategy into action through the power of content marketing. This chapter, "Social Media Content Marketing," equips you with the knowledge and tools to create engaging content that resonates with your audience across different platforms.

In the realm of social media, content is king. It's the fuel that ignites conversations, fosters brand loyalty, and ultimately drives results. But with so much content vying for attention, how do you make yours stand out? The key lies in understanding your audience, tailoring your content to specific platforms, and crafting stories that truly connect.

### Content Pillars: The Foundation of Your Strategy

Before diving into specific content formats, establish your content pillars – the core themes and topics that will guide your content creation. These pillars should be relevant to your brand, resonate with your target audience, and align with your overall marketing objectives.

Here are some questions to consider when defining your content pillars:

• What are your brand's core values and mission?
• What are your audience's interests and pain points?
• What type of content aligns with your social media goals (brand awareness, lead generation, etc.)?

For example, if you're a company selling fitness apparel, your content pillars might include healthy living tips, workout routines, inspirational stories, and product showcases.

**Content Variety is the Spice of Life** (and Social Media)

Once you've established your content pillars, it's time to explore the diverse landscape of social media content formats. Don't get stuck in a rut! Mix things up by incorporating a variety of formats to keep your audience engaged:

• Blog Posts: Share informative and insightful blog posts that provide valuable content to your audience.

- Images:  Eye-catching visuals are essential for grabbing attention and conveying messages quickly. Use high-quality images, infographics, and memes.
- Videos:  Videos are a powerful tool for storytelling, showcasing products, and demonstrating tutorials. Utilize short-form video formats like Instagram Reels and TikTok to maximize reach.
- Live Videos:  Host live Q&A sessions, product demonstrations, or behind-the-scenes glimpses to connect with your audience in real-time.
- Stories:  Leverage disappearing story features on platforms like Instagram and Facebook to share snippets of your day, offer sneak peeks, or run interactive polls.

By experimenting with different formats, you can discover what resonates best with your audience on each platform.

## The Power of Storytelling: Connecting on an Emotional Level

Don't just inform, inspire!  Weave storytelling into your content to connect with your audience on a deeper level.  People are drawn to narratives, so use them to showcase your brand values, highlight customer experiences, and evoke emotions.

Here are some tips for incorporating storytelling into your social media content:

• Focus on characters:  Create relatable characters that your audience can connect with.

• Craft a narrative arc:  Every story needs a beginning, middle, and end.  Hook your audience with an enticing intro, build suspense, and deliver a satisfying conclusion.

• Evoke emotions:  Make your audience laugh, cry, or feel inspired through your storytelling.

• Use visuals strategically:  Images and videos can amplify the emotional impact of your stories.

By weaving compelling narratives into your content, you'll forge a stronger emotional connection with your audience and leave a lasting impression.

**Tailoring Content for Different Platforms: Understanding Nuances**

Remember, each social media platform has its own unique audience and content preferences.  Here's a quick guide to tailoring your content for some popular platforms:

• Facebook:  Longer-form content like blog posts and informative articles perform well alongside eye-catching visuals.

• Instagram:   High-quality photos and short-form videos (Reels) reign supreme.  Focus on aesthetics and lifestyle content.

- Twitter: Concise, newsworthy content and real-time updates are key. Utilize hashtags effectively to join conversations.
- LinkedIn: Professional and informative content related to your industry is essential. Share industry insights, articles, and thought leadership pieces.

By understanding the nuances of each platform, you can tailor your content for maximum impact and engagement.

Remember, social media content marketing is an ongoing process. Experiment, analyze your results, and adapt your content strategy to keep your audience coming back for more!

# Chapter-4

## Content Calendar and Scheduling: Mastering the Art of Consistency

This chapter, "Content Calendar and Scheduling," equips you with the tools and techniques to develop a streamlined content calendar and master the art of social media scheduling.

Imagine a social media presence without a plan – a flurry of last-minute posts and missed opportunities. A content calendar is your roadmap to success, ensuring consistent content flow, strategic timing, and alignment with your overall marketing goals.

### Building Your Content Calendar: A Symphony of Planning

A well-crafted content calendar acts as a central hub for organizing your social media content. Here's a breakdown of the key elements to include:

- Content Pillars: Refer back to your established content pillars to guide your content themes for each week/month.
- Content Formats: Plan the mix of content formats (text, images, videos) you'll be using for each post.

- Posting Schedule:  Determine the frequency and timing of your posts for each platform, considering peak engagement times.
- Platform-Specific Content: Tailor content to the specific requirements and audience preferences of each platform.
- Calls to Action (CTAs):  Include clear CTAs in your posts to encourage engagement (e.g., "Like this post," "Visit our website").
- Holidays and Events:  Leverage seasonal trends and upcoming holidays to create relevant and timely content.
- Visuals and Hashtags:  Plan visuals and relevant hashtags to accompany each post to enhance reach and discoverability.

"Pro Tip": Utilize content calendar templates readily available online or create your own using spreadsheets or project management tools.

## Scheduling Like a Pro: Tools and Techniques for Efficiency

Once your content calendar is in place, leverage social media scheduling tools to streamline your workflow and ensure consistent posting.  Here are some popular scheduling tools to consider:

- Hootsuite
- Buffer
- Sprout Social
- Later

• Meta Business Suite (for Facebook and Instagram)

These tools allow you to schedule posts across multiple platforms in advance, saving you time and ensuring consistent content flow. However, remember that scheduling is not a substitute for real-time engagement. Be sure to monitor your platforms and respond to comments and messages promptly.

**Mastering the Art of Consistency: Reap the Rewards**

Here's why a consistent posting schedule is crucial for social media success:

• Builds Brand Awareness: Regular posting keeps your brand top-of-mind with your audience.
• Fosters Engagement: Consistent content prompts interaction and encourages audience participation.
• Drives Results: Regularly scheduled content paves the way for achieving your social media goals, be it brand awareness, lead generation, or website traffic.

Remember, consistency is key! By planning your content calendar and scheduling posts in advance, you'll establish a rhythm for your social media presence, optimize your workflow, and ultimately achieve your marketing objectives.

# Chapter-5

## Understanding Social Media Platforms: Mastering the Nuances of Each Network

Throughout this chapter, we've explored the strategic side of social media marketing – crafting a winning strategy, creating compelling content, and maintaining consistent scheduling.  Now, it's time to delve into the world of the platforms themselves.  This chapter, "Understanding Social Media Platforms," equips you with the knowledge and expertise to navigate the unique features and functionalities of the major social media landscapes.

Think of social media platforms as your toolbox – each with its own set of tools specifically designed to achieve different goals.  Understanding the strengths and nuances of each platform allows you to tailor your approach and maximize engagement with your target audience.  Here's a breakdown of some of the most popular social media platforms and their key characteristics:

## 1. Facebook:

• The OG Social Network:  Still the leading platform in terms of user base, Facebook caters to a broad demographic.
• Content Powerhouse:  Supports a variety of content formats – text, images, videos, live streams, and long-form articles.
• Community Building:  Ideal for fostering brand communities through groups and discussions.
• Paid Advertising:  Offers robust advertising options for targeted reach and campaign optimization.

"Pro Tip: Utilize Facebook groups to engage with niche audiences and establish yourself as a thought leader in your industry.

## 2. Instagram:

• The Realm of Aesthetics:  A visually-driven platform where high-quality photos and short-form videos (Reels) reign supreme.
• Influencer Marketing Hub:  A popular platform for influencer marketing campaigns.
• Storytelling Through Snapshots:  Leverage Instagram Stories to share glimpses of your day, behind-the-scenes content, and interactive polls.

• Shoppable Posts: Sell products directly through shoppable posts, making it a powerful tool for e-commerce businesses.

"Pro Tip: Utilize eye-catching visuals, relevant hashtags, and strategic geotags to maximize reach and discovery on Instagram.

### 3. Twitter:

• The Pulse of What's Happening: A real-time platform ideal for sharing news updates, breaking trends, and customer service interactions.
• Conversation Starter: Foster discussions and participate in trending conversations using relevant hashtags.
• Concise is King: Content on Twitter thrives on brevity and quick updates.
• Thought Leadership Platform: Share industry insights, articles, and engage with thought leaders in your field.

"Pro Tip: Monitor trending hashtags and participate in relevant conversations to increase brand awareness and connect with potential customers on Twitter.

### 4. LinkedIn:

• The Professional Network: The go-to platform for professional networking, B2B marketing, and employer branding.

• Content Marketing Playground: Share industry insights, articles, and establish yourself as a thought leader in your field.

• Job Hunting Haven: Utilize LinkedIn to connect with potential employers and showcase your professional profile.

• Networking Groups: Join relevant LinkedIn groups to connect with industry professionals and participate in discussions.

"Pro Tip: Publish long-form content like articles on LinkedIn to establish yourself as an authority in your field and attract potential clients.

## 5. TikTok:

• The Rise of Short-Form Video: A rapidly growing platform focused on short-form, engaging video content.

• Entertainment is Key: Create fun, informative, or entertaining videos to capture attention and go viral.

• Influencer Marketing Potential: A platform gaining traction for influencer marketing campaigns.

• Geofencing and Targeting: Leverage location-based targeting to reach specific demographics within a particular area.

"Pro Tip: Experiment with different video formats, trending sounds, and challenges to gain traction and build a following on TikTok.

Remember, this is not an exhaustive list! The social media landscape is constantly evolving, with new platforms emerging all the time. Staying updated on the latest trends and adapting your approach accordingly is crucial for success.

# Chapter -6

## Social Media Advertising: Boosting Your Reach and Results

So far, we've explored the foundation of social media marketing – crafting a winning strategy, creating engaging content, and mastering different platforms. Now, it's time to delve into the world of paid advertising, a powerful tool to amplify your reach and achieve your marketing goals on social media. This chapter, "Social Media Advertising," equips you with the knowledge and skills to navigate the exciting realm of paid social media campaigns.

Organic content creation is essential for building brand awareness and fostering relationships with your audience. However, in today's crowded social media landscape, organic reach can be limited. This is where social media advertising comes in – a targeted approach to reach a wider audience, drive specific actions, and ultimately achieve your marketing objectives.

**Unveiling the Power of Paid Advertising:**

Here's how social media advertising can benefit your brand:

• Increased Brand Awareness:  Reach a wider audience beyond your organic followers and get your brand in front of potential customers.

• Targeted Reach:  Precise targeting options allow you to reach users based on demographics, interests, behaviors, and online activity.

• Specific Actionable Goals:  Design campaigns to achieve specific goals, such as website traffic, lead generation, app downloads, or product sales.

• Measurable Results:  Track the performance of your campaigns in real-time and measure your return on investment (ROI).

• Boost Engagement:  Paid advertising can help promote your organic content, leading to increased engagement and brand visibility.

Think of social media advertising as a targeted rocket booster for your social media strategy, propelling your content and brand message to a wider audience.

**Understanding The Advertising Landscape:**

Here's a breakdown of the key elements involved in social media advertising:

• Campaign Objectives:  Define your clear goals – do you want to increase brand awareness, generate leads, or drive website traffic?

• Targeting Options:  Leverage demographic, interest-based, and behavioral targeting to reach the right audience.

• Budget and Bidding:  Set a budget for your campaign and choose a bidding strategy that aligns with your goals (e.g., cost per click, cost per impression).

• Ad Formats:  Select the most suitable ad format for your campaign (e.g., image ads, video ads, carousel ads)

• Landing Pages:  Direct users to conversion-optimized landing pages that align with your campaign goals.

• Tracking and Analytics:  Monitor the performance of your campaigns, analyze results, and make data-driven optimizations.

Each social media platform offers its own advertising platform with unique features and functionalities.  We'll explore these in detail in the upcoming chapters.

**Campaign Best Practices:**

Here are some key tips for running successful social media ad campaigns:

• Start with a clear objective:  Always define your goals upfront to ensure your campaign is aligned with your overall social media strategy.

- Know your target audience:  Precise targeting is crucial for maximizing your campaign's effectiveness.
- Craft compelling ad copy:  Write clear, concise, and engaging ad copy that grabs attention and motivates action.
- Utilize high-quality visuals:  Eye-catching visuals are essential for stopping users in their scroll and capturing their interest.
- Track and analyze results:  Monitor your campaign performance and make adjustments based on data insights.
- Test and iterate:  Experiment with different ad formats, targeting options, and creatives to optimize your campaigns for better results.

By following these best practices and staying updated on the latest advertising trends, you can create high-performing social media ad campaigns that deliver a significant return on investment.

# Chapter -7

## Social Media Community Management and Engagement: Building Thriving Online Communities

We've explored crafting a winning social media strategy, creating engaging content, and navigating the advertising landscape. Now, it's time to delve into the heart of social media success – building and managing vibrant online communities. This chapter, "Community Management and Engagement," equips you with the skills and knowledge to foster brand loyalty, cultivate meaningful relationships, and turn your social media audience into a thriving community.

Social media is more than just broadcasting messages – it's about creating a space for conversation, connection, and shared experiences. A strong community around your brand fosters brand loyalty, amplifies your reach through word-of-mouth marketing, and provides valuable customer insights.

## The Art of Community Building:

Here's how to cultivate a thriving social media community:

- Define Your Audience:  Understand who your target audience is and what kind of community they would value.
- Establish a Brand Voice:  Develop a consistent and engaging brand voice that resonates with your community.
- Create Valuable Content:  Share content that informs, entertains, and inspires your audience, encouraging interaction.
- Respond Promptly:  Actively participate in conversations, respond to comments and messages promptly, and address concerns effectively.
- Run Contests and Giveaways:  Host interactive contests and giveaways to generate excitement and encourage participation.
- Recognize and Reward Engagement:  Show appreciation to your community members for their likes, comments, and shares.
- Facilitate Discussions:  Pose questions, spark conversations, and encourage healthy debate on relevant topics within your niche.
- Utilize Social Listening Tools:  Monitor brand mentions and conversations happening online to stay connected with your audience.

By implementing these strategies, you'll foster a sense of belonging and encourage your audience to become active participants in your online community.

**Engagement Strategies: Keeping the Conversation Flowing**

Here are some specific techniques to keep your social media community engaged:

• Run polls and surveys: Gather valuable insights from your audience and spark discussions based on their responses.
• Host live Q&A sessions: Connect with your audience in real-time, answer their questions, and build a more personal connection.
• Partner with influencers: Collaborate with relevant influencers to reach a wider audience and leverage their credibility.
• Feature user-generated content: Showcase content created by your audience (photos, videos, testimonials) to build trust and encourage participation.
• Run social media challenges: Create engaging challenges that encourage user participation and brand interaction.

By implementing these engagement strategies, you'll keep your audience interested, coming back for more, and actively participating in your online community.

**The Power of Community Management Tools:**

Several social media management tools can streamline your community management efforts:

• Sprout Social
• Hootsuite
• Buffer
• Mention
• Brandwatch

These tools allow you to schedule posts, monitor brand mentions, engage with followers across platforms, and analyze community sentiment.

  Remember, community management is an ongoing process!  It requires dedication, responsiveness, and a genuine desire to connect with your audience.  By consistently implementing these strategies and fostering a positive online environment, you'll build a loyal community that becomes a valuable asset for your brand.

# Chapter -8

## Unveiling the Power of Data: Social Media Analytics and Reporting

Throughout this chapter, you've explored the strategic and creative aspects of social media marketing – crafting a winning strategy, creating compelling content, fostering vibrant communities, and navigating the advertising landscape. Now, it's time to delve into the world of data analysis. This chapter, "Social Media Analytics and Reporting," equips you with the tools and knowledge to measure your social media performance, translate data into actionable insights, and demonstrate the value of your social media efforts to stakeholders.

Social media isn't just about posting and hoping for the best. It's about understanding what resonates with your audience, what drives results, and ultimately, measuring the effectiveness of your strategies. Data empowers you to make informed decisions, optimize your campaigns, and achieve your social media goals.

### Key Performance Indicators (KPIs): Measuring What Matters

The first step to social media analytics is identifying the right Key Performance Indicators (KPIs) to track. These metrics will vary depending on your specific goals, but here are some common social media KPIs to consider:

• Brand Awareness: Reach, impressions, follower growth, brand mentions.
• Engagement: Likes, comments, shares, clicks, participation in polls and contests.
• Website Traffic: Click-through rates (CTRs) from social media to your website.
• Lead Generation: Number of leads generated through social media campaigns.
• Sales: Conversions generated from social media efforts (e-commerce tracking).

By tracking these KPIs, you can measure the impact of your social media efforts and identify areas for improvement.

### Demystifying Social Media Analytics Tools:

Most social media platforms offer built-in analytics dashboards that provide valuable insights into your audience and content performance. Here are some popular platforms and their analytics features:

• Facebook Insights: Provides data on reach, engagement, demographics of your audience, and performance of paid advertising campaigns.

• Instagram Insights: Offers insights into follower demographics, engagement metrics, and performance of Instagram Stories and Reels.
• Twitter Analytics: Tracks tweet impressions, engagement rates, mentions, and website clicks.
• LinkedIn Analytics: Provides data on post reach, engagement, follower demographics, and website traffic generated from LinkedIn.

In addition to platform-specific tools, consider using social media management platforms like Hootsuite or Sprout Social that offer comprehensive analytics dashboards for all your social media channels in one place.

**Crafting Compelling Social Media Reports:**

Social media analytics data is powerful, but to truly demonstrate the value of your social media efforts, you need to translate that data into a compelling story for stakeholders. Here's how to craft effective social media reports:

• Define Your Audience: Tailor your report to the needs and interests of your audience (e.g., executives, marketing team).
• Set Clear Goals: Outline the specific goals you were trying to achieve with your social media efforts.
• Highlight Key Metrics: Present the most relevant KPIs that demonstrate progress towards your goals.

• Visualize Your Data: Utilize charts, graphs, and infographics to make your data visually appealing and easier to understand.

• Show the Impact: Demonstrate how social media is contributing to your overall marketing objectives (e.g., increased brand awareness, lead generation).

• Offer Actionable Insights: Conclude your report with actionable recommendations for improvement based on your data analysis.

By following these steps, you can create social media reports that showcase the effectiveness of your efforts and drive strategic decision-making within your organization.

**Embrace the Power of Data-Driven Decisions:**

Social media analytics empowers you to:

• Optimize Your Content Strategy: Identify what content resonates best with your audience and adjust your content calendar accordingly.

• Target Your Audience More Effectively: Utilize audience insights to refine your targeting strategies for both organic and paid campaigns.

• Measure ROI (Return on Investment): Demonstrate the value of your social media efforts by tracking conversions and sales generated through your social media channels.

• Stay Ahead of the Curve:  Monitor industry trends and adapt your social media strategy based on data-driven insights.

By embracing data analysis and reporting, you can transform your social media efforts from guesswork to a strategic and measurable approach that delivers real results.

Remember, the social media landscape is constantly evolving.  Stay curious, keep learning, and adapt your strategies to stay ahead of the curve.  By combining creativity, data analysis, and a genuine passion for connecting with your audience, you'll be well on your way to social media.

# Chapter -9

## Social Media Crisis Management: Navigating the Unexpected with Confidence

Throughout this article, you've conquered the art of crafting a social media strategy, engaging your audience, and measuring your success. Now, let's delve into the realm of the unexpected – social media crisis management. This chapter equips you with the knowledge and tools to navigate public controversies, negative comments, and unforeseen circumstances with grace and effectiveness.

Social media, with its lightning-fast spread of information, can turn a minor misstep into a full-blown crisis. But fear not! By having a plan in place and acting swiftly, you can minimize damage, protect your brand reputation, and even emerge from the situation stronger.

### The Looming Threat: Identifying Potential Crises

The first step is recognizing potential threats lurking on the social media horizon. Here are some common social media crises to consider:

• Product Issues: Safety concerns, malfunctioning products, or negative customer experiences can spark outrage online.

• Public Relations Blunders: Offensive marketing campaigns, insensitive remarks, or ethical controversies can damage your brand image.

• Data Breaches: Customer privacy breaches can severely erode trust in your brand.

• Employee Misconduct: Inappropriate social media posts or actions by employees can reflect poorly on your company.

• Fake News or Rumors: The spread of misinformation online can create confusion and damage your reputation.

By anticipating these potential issues, you can develop a crisis communication plan to address them effectively.

**Building Your Crisis Fortress: The Essential Plan**

A well-defined crisis communication plan acts as your roadmap during a social media storm. Here's what to include:

• Crisis Team: Assemble a dedicated team responsible for managing the crisis, including representatives from PR, marketing, legal, and customer service.

• Communication Protocols:  Establish clear guidelines for who speaks for the brand on social media during a crisis.
• Monitoring Tools: Utilize social listening tools to track brand mentions and identify emerging issues promptly.
• Draft Statements: Prepare pre-approved templates for potential crisis scenarios to expedite communication.
• Review and Update:** Regularly review and update your crisis communication plan to ensure its effectiveness.

Remember, a crisis plan is only as good as its execution. Regularly conduct training exercises to ensure your team is prepared to act swiftly and cohesively when a crisis strikes.

## The Art of Crisis Communication: Responding with Authenticity

When a crisis hits, clear and timely communication is paramount. Here are some key principles for crisis communication on social media:

• Acknowledge the Issue:  Address the situation head-on and avoid brushing it under the rug.
• Emphasize Transparency:  Be honest and transparent about the situation, even if all the details are not available.

• Express Empathy:  Acknowledge the concerns of your audience and show empathy for those affected.

• Communicate Regularly:  Provide updates and take responsibility for addressing the issue.

• Be Authentic:  Maintain a genuine and sincere brand voice throughout your communication.

Social media allows for two-way communication. Actively listen to your audience, respond to comments and messages, and address concerns promptly. This demonstrates that you value your audience and are committed to resolving the issue.

**Learning from the Storm: Post-Crisis Evaluation**

Once the dust settles, take time to analyze the crisis and its aftermath. Here's what you can do:

• Review Your Response:  Evaluate the effectiveness of your crisis communication strategy. Identify areas for improvement for future situations.

• Gather Feedback:  Seek feedback from your audience and stakeholders to understand their perception of your crisis management.

• Refine Your Plan:  Based on the evaluation, update your crisis communication plan to address any shortcomings.

By learning from each crisis, you can strengthen your brand's resilience and emerge from challenging situations with a renewed sense of trust and loyalty from your audience.

Remember, social media crisis management is not about shielding negativity; it's about demonstrating your brand's commitment to transparency, accountability, and open communication. By being prepared and acting with integrity, you can weather any social media storm and solidify your brand's reputation.

# Chapter-10

## Staying Ahead of the Curve: Mastering the Ever-Evolving Social Media Landscape

Congratulations, social media maven! You've conquered the core concepts of social media management, from crafting a winning strategy to navigating the intricacies of crisis communication. But the social media landscape is a dynamic beast, constantly evolving and presenting new opportunities and challenges. This chapter, "Staying Ahead of the Curve," equips you with the tools and mindset to future-proof your skills and ensure you remain at the forefront of social media trends.

The digital world thrives on innovation. New platforms emerge, content formats gain traction, and user behaviors shift. As a social media manager, staying ahead of the curve requires a commitment to continuous learning and a willingness to adapt your strategies to the ever-changing ecosystem.

## Future-Proofing Your Skills: A Growth Mindset

Here are some key practices to cultivate a growth mindset and stay relevant in the social media world:

• Embrace Lifelong Learning:  Dedicate time to continuous learning.  Subscribe to industry publications, attend webinars and conferences, and explore online courses to stay updated on the latest trends and best practices.
• Become a Social Media News Junkie:  Follow thought leaders, influencers, and industry publications on social media to stay abreast of emerging trends and news in real-time.
• Experimentation is Key:  Don't be afraid to experiment with new features, platforms, and content formats.  Test and analyze the results to see what resonates with your audience.
• Embrace New Technologies:  Educate yourself on emerging technologies like artificial intelligence (AI), augmented reality (AR), and virtual reality (VR) to understand their potential impact on social media marketing.
• Network with Your Peers:  Connect with other social media professionals online and offline to share knowledge, exchange ideas, and stay inspired.

By actively seeking out new information and fostering a growth mindset, you'll equip yourself with the skills and knowledge to thrive in the ever-evolving social media landscape.

**The Crystal Ball of Social Media: Trends to Watch**

While predicting the future is impossible, here are some current trends shaping the social media landscape to keep on your radar:

• The Rise of Short-Form Video: Platforms like TikTok and Instagram Reels are captivating audiences with short, engaging video content. Consider incorporating short-form video into your content strategy.
• The Power of Influencer Marketing: Partnering with relevant influencers can be a powerful way to reach new audiences and build brand credibility.
• The Era of Social Commerce: Social media platforms are increasingly integrating shopping functionalities. Explore features like shoppable posts and live commerce to drive sales directly through social media.
• The Humanization of Brands: Consumers connect with brands that have a human touch. Showcase your brand personality and connect with your audience on a deeper level through storytelling and user-generated content.
• The Importance of Social Listening: Utilize social listening tools to monitor brand mentions, understand audience sentiment, and identify trending topics to inform your content strategy.

By understanding these trends and staying updated on emerging technologies, you'll be well-positioned to adapt your strategies and capitalize on new opportunities within the social media landscape.

The world of social media is a thrilling adventure, full of challenges and opportunities. By staying curious, embracing continuous learning, and adapting your strategies to the ever-evolving landscape, you'll not only survive in this dynamic space, but thrive and become a true social media master!

The social media landscape is constantly changing, but the core principles you've learned here will remain constant. Use this knowledge as a springboard to launch your social media management career or elevate your brand's social presence. Don't be afraid to step outside your comfort zone, embrace challenges, and become a true social media guru.

# Chapter-11

## Developing a Winning Social Media Strategy

Social media has become an undeniable force in today's digital landscape. For businesses of all sizes, it presents a powerful opportunity to connect with audiences, build brand awareness, and achieve marketing goals. But simply having a social media presence isn't enough. To truly thrive, you need a winning social media strategy.

This chapter module will equip you with the knowledge and tools to develop and implement effective social media strategies. We'll delve into each crucial step, from defining your goals to measuring success.

### Step 1: Setting SMART Goals

Every successful social media strategy starts with a clear understanding of what you want to achieve. Formulate Specific, Measurable, Achievable, Relevant, and Time-Bound (SMART) goals.

• Specific: Clearly define what you want to accomplish. Increase brand awareness? Drive website traffic? Generate leads?

- Measurable: Establish metrics to track progress. This could be follower growth, engagement rate (likes, comments, shares), website clicks, or lead conversions.
- Achievable: Be realistic about what you can achieve within a timeframe.
- Relevant: Ensure your goals align with your overall marketing objectives and business strategy.
- Time-Bound: Set a timeframe for achieving your goals.

### Step 2: Knowing Your Audience

Understanding your target audience is fundamental to crafting compelling social media content. Conduct thorough research to create detailed buyer personas. Consider demographics, interests, online behavior, and the platforms they frequent.

### Step 3: Competitive Analysis

Research your competitors in the social media space. Analyze their profiles, content strategy, and audience engagement. Identify their strengths and weaknesses to find opportunities to differentiate your brand.

### Step 4: Choosing the Right Channels

Don't spread yourself too thin. Focus on the platforms where your target audience is most active. Consider factors like platform demographics, content formats, and your overall marketing goals.

### Step 5: Crafting Engaging Content

Content is king (or queen) on social media. Develop a strategy to create high-quality content that resonates with your audience. This could include blog posts, images, infographics, videos, live streams, and user-generated content.

- Prioritize value: Inform, educate, or entertain your audience.
- Maintain brand consistency: Ensure your content reflects your brand voice and identity.
- Experiment with different formats: Cater to diverse preferences and maximize reach.
- Post consistently: Maintain a regular posting schedule to stay top-of-mind.

Step 6: Building Community and Engagement

Social media is a two-way street. Foster a sense of community and encourage engagement. Respond to comments and messages promptly, run contests and giveaways, and participate in relevant conversations.

### Step 7: Analyzing and Adapting

Track your progress using social media analytics tools. Monitor key metrics and identify what's working and what's not. Be prepared to adapt your strategy based on data insights and audience feedback.

"Bonus Tip:  Embrace Social Media Management Tools

Several social media management tools can streamline your workflow and boost efficiency. Explore options for scheduling posts, managing multiple accounts, and analyzing performance data.

By following these steps and continuously refining your approach, you can develop a winning social media strategy that delivers real results for your brand. Remember, social media is a marathon, not a sprint. Be patient, stay focused, and  keep learning to stay ahead of the curve.

# Chapter-12

## Creating Engaging Content for Different Platforms: Mastering the Social Media Landscape

In today's social media sphere, capturing audience attention requires content that's not just informative, but truly engaging. This course module will equip you with the knowledge to tailor content for each platform, maximizing reach and fostering meaningful connections.

### Understanding Platform Specifics

Each social media platform has its own unique characteristics and target audience. Optimizing your content for each platform is key to maximizing engagement. Here's a breakdown of some popular platforms:

• Facebook: Ideal for sharing long-form content like articles, infographics, and live videos. Encourage discussions with polls and questions.
• Instagram: A visual platform that thrives on high-quality images and short videos. Leverage Instagram Stories for ephemeral content and highlights for curated collections.

• Twitter:  Fast-paced and text-driven. Focus on concise, attention-grabbing posts with relevant hashtags.  Run Twitter chats and participate in trending conversations.

• LinkedIn:  Professional networking platform. Share industry-related articles, infographics, and thought leadership pieces. Engage with discussions in relevant groups.

• YouTube:  The go-to platform for video content. Create informative tutorials, product demos, and behind-the-scenes glimpses. Optimize titles and descriptions with relevant keywords.

• TikTok: Short-form video platform known for its viral trends and challenges. Create engaging and creative videos that capture attention within seconds.

## Content Tailoring Tips

• Length:  Adhere to platform-specific norms. Keep it concise on Twitter, while allowing for more depth on Facebook or LinkedIn.

• Visuals:  Prioritize high-quality visuals across all platforms.  Utilize eye-catching images, infographics, and captivating video snippets.

• Voice & Tone: Adapt your brand voice to suit the platform's personality. Maintain a professional tone on LinkedIn, while fostering a more casual and conversational approach on Twitter or Instagram.

• Hashtags:  Use relevant hashtags to increase discoverability on platforms like Twitter and

Instagram. Research trending hashtags and incorporate them strategically.

• Calls to Action (CTAs): Tell your audience what you want them to do next. Whether it's visiting your website, subscribing to your channel, or joining a discussion, clear CTAs drive engagement.

### Engaging Content Formats

• Images & Graphics: Eye-catching visuals are essential for grabbing attention. Use high-quality photos, infographics, and design elements that complement your brand identity.

• Videos: Video content is king across most platforms. Leverage explainer videos, product demos, customer testimonials, and behind-the-scenes glimpses to connect with your audience. Explore live streaming features for real-time engagement.

• Stories: Ephemeral content formats like Instagram and Facebook Stories allow for a more personal and interactive experience. Share behind-the-scenes snippets, polls, quizzes, and questions to spark conversation.

• User-Generated Content (UGC): Encourage your audience to create and share content related to your brand. Run contests, giveaways, and challenges to leverage the power of UGC and foster a sense of community.

Remember:

• Consistency is Key: Maintain a regular posting schedule to stay top-of-mind and build anticipation.

• Experiment and Analyze: Don't be afraid to experiment with different formats and content types. Track your results and adapt your strategy based on what resonates with your audience.

• Stay Updated: Social media trends and algorithms are constantly evolving. Stay informed about platform updates and adapt your approach accordingly.

By understanding these principles and continuously refining your content strategy for each platform, you can become a master of social media content creation, fostering a community around your brand and achieving your marketing goals.

# Chapter-13

## Scheduling and Publishing Posts for Social Media Success: Mastering Your Time and Reach

In the fast-paced world of social media, consistency is crucial. But manually posting across multiple platforms can be a time-consuming hassle. This chapter module will equip you with strategies and tools to effectively schedule and publish your social media content, maximizing efficiency and reach.

### The Power of Scheduling

Scheduling your social media posts in advance offers numerous advantages:

• Saves Time:  Plan your content calendar in advance and free yourself up for other tasks.
• Consistency:  Maintain a regular posting schedule to stay top-of-mind with your audience.
• Strategic Posting:  Schedule posts for optimal times when your audience is most active.
• Collaboration:  Streamline workflows by scheduling posts for team review and approval.

## Building a Content Calendar

The foundation for effective scheduling lies in a well-defined content calendar. Here's how to create yours:

• Identify Key Dates:  Mark important industry events, holidays, and promotional campaigns.
• Content Mix:  Plan a variety of content formats like images, videos, articles, and live streams.
• Platform Specifics:  Tailor content and posting times for each social media platform.
• Visual Appeal:  Include visuals for each post in your calendar, ensuring a cohesive brand aesthetic.
• Scheduling Tools:  Utilize built-in scheduling features or social media management tools.

## Choosing the Right Time to Post

Timing plays a significant role in social media reach and engagement. Here are some tips:

• Research Platform Insights:  Most platforms offer analytics tools that reveal peak activity times for your audience.  Schedule posts accordingly.
• Industry Benchmarks:  Research general best practices for posting times within your industry.
• Experiment and Analyze:  Track your results and adjust posting times based on what resonates best with your audience.

## Scheduling and Publishing Tools

Several social media management tools can streamline your scheduling workflow:

• Built-in Scheduling:  Most major social media platforms offer native scheduling features.
• Social Media Management Tools:  Third-party tools offer advanced scheduling functionalities, bulk posting options, and content library management.
• Content Calendars:  Integrate social media scheduling with online calendar tools for a holistic overview of your marketing activities.

## Effective Publishing Practices

Even with a well-scheduled plan, remember these publishing best practices:

• Proofread & Edit:  Double-check your posts for typos and grammatical errors before publishing.
• Engage with Comments:  Respond to comments and messages promptly to foster a sense of community.
• Monitor Performance:  Track key metrics like reach, engagement, and click-through rates to measure success.
• Be Flexible:  Adjust your schedule as needed based on real-time events or trending topics.

By mastering scheduling and publishing techniques, you'll free up valuable time, ensure consistent brand presence, and maximize your reach on social media. Remember, a well-planned and efficiently managed content calendar is a social media manager's secret weapon!

# Chapter-14

## How to Analyze Social Media Data and Track Your Progress

In today's data-driven marketing landscape, social media analytics are the compass guiding your strategy. This chapter module will equip you with the knowledge and tools to effectively analyze social media data, track your progress, and make data-driven decisions to optimize your social media presence.

### Why Analyze Social Media Data?

Social media data holds a wealth of information about your audience, content performance, and overall campaign effectiveness. Analyzing this data empowers you to:

• Measure Success: Track progress towards your defined SMART goals (Specific, Measurable, Achievable, Relevant, and Time-Bound).
• Understand Your Audience: Gain insights into demographics, interests, and online behavior to refine your targeting strategies.
• Evaluate Content Performance: Identify what content resonates with your audience and what needs improvement.

• Identify Trends: Discover emerging trends and adapt your content strategy to capitalize on them.

• Optimize Your Approach: Make data-driven decisions to improve reach, engagement, and achieve your social media objectives.

## Key Metrics to Track

Different metrics offer valuable insights depending on your goals. Here are some key metrics to consider:

• Reach: The number of unique users who saw your content.

• Engagement: Likes, comments, shares, saves, and other actions users take on your posts.

• Click-Through Rate (CTR): The percentage of users who click on a link within your post.

• Conversions: The number of users who take a desired action after seeing your content (e.g., sign-ups, purchases).

• Brand Mentions: Instances where your brand is mentioned online, even if it's not on your profiles directly.

• Follower Growth: The rate at which your audience expands.

• Sentiment Analysis: The overall sentiment (positive, negative, or neutral) expressed in audience comments and mentions.

## Essential Social Media Analytics Tools

Most social media platforms offer built-in analytics dashboards. Here's a breakdown:

• Facebook Insights: Provides detailed data on reach, engagement, demographics, and website traffic generated from your Facebook page.
• Twitter Analytics: Offers insights into impressions, engagement, follower demographics, and link clicks.
• Instagram Insights: Analyzes profile views, reach, engagement, and website clicks driven by your Instagram content.
• LinkedIn Analytics: Provides data on post performance, audience demographics, and website clicks.
• YouTube Analytics: Offers in-depth data on video views, watch time, audience demographics, and subscriber growth.
• Social Media Management Tools: Many third-party tools offer comprehensive analytics features across all major platforms, allowing for unified reporting and data visualization.

## Advanced Social Media Listening Techniques

Social media listening goes beyond basic analytics. Utilize tools that track brand mentions across the web, including social media platforms, blogs, and forums. This allows you to:

• Identify brand sentiment: Understand how your audience perceives your brand.
• Discover customer feedback: Gain valuable insights into customer satisfaction and areas for improvement.
• Monitor industry trends: Stay informed about industry conversations and emerging topics.
• Engage in crisis management: Respond promptly to negative mentions and address customer concerns.

## Turning Data into Actionable Insights

Once you've gathered data, the key lies in translating it into actionable insights. Here are some steps:

• Set Benchmarks: Establish reference points to track your progress over time.
• Identify Trends: Look for patterns and recurring themes in your data.
• Compare Performance: Benchmark your performance against industry averages or your own historical data.
• A/B Testing: Test different content formats and posting times to identify what works best.
• Refine Your Strategy: Adapt your content strategy, target audience, and posting schedule based on your findings.

Remember, social media data analysis is an ongoing process. Continuously monitor your metrics, experiment with different approaches, and adapt your strategy to maximize your social media success. By harnessing the power of data, you can transform your social media presence into a measurable and impactful marketing channel.

# Chapter-15

## How to Manage Social Media Communities and Respond to Comments and Messages

Social media isn't just about broadcasting messages; it's about fostering a thriving community. This chapter module will equip you with the skills to effectively manage social media communities, fostering meaningful connections and building brand loyalty through thoughtful responses to comments and messages.

### Building a Vibrant Community

• Define Your Community Guidelines: Establish clear expectations for respectful and productive discussions. Outline what content is considered inappropriate and your approach to moderation.

• Encourage Participation: Spark conversations by asking open-ended questions, running polls, and hosting contests.

• Recognize and Reward Engagement: Show appreciation for user-generated content, comments, and shares.

• Embrace Authenticity: Respond with a genuine and human voice that reflects your brand personality.

• Facilitate Connections:  Encourage interaction between community members by tagging relevant users in conversations.

## Responding to Comments and Messages

• Promptness is Key:  Strive to respond to comments and messages promptly, demonstrating that you value your audience's engagement.
• Personalize Your Responses:  Avoid generic responses. Tailor your messages to acknowledge the specific comment or question.
• Address Concerns Promptly:  Don't shy away from negative comments. Address them professionally and offer solutions when possible.
• Maintain a Positive Tone:  Even when addressing negativity, strive to maintain a courteous and helpful approach.
• Utilize Different Response Formats:  For simple questions, a quick response within the comments section might suffice. For complex inquiries, consider taking the conversation private through direct message.

## Advanced Community Management Techniques

• Identify Community Champions:  Recognize and empower active and positive members who contribute valuable insights and discussions.
• Host Live Events:  Engage your audience in real-time through live Q&A sessions, product demos, or behind-the-scenes glimpses.

• Utilize Social Listening Tools:  Monitor brand mentions beyond your profiles to identify conversations and engage with potential customers.

• Run Targeted Campaigns:  Leverage social media advertising platforms to reach specific audience segments within your community and promote relevant content or offers.

## Building a Community Management Workflow

• Establish a Monitoring Schedule:  Dedicate specific times throughout the day to check comments and messages across all platforms.

• Utilize Social Media Management Tools:  Many tools offer features to manage messages from various platforms in a centralized location.

• Develop Response Templates:  Create pre-written templates for common questions or concerns to save time while maintaining a personalized touch.

• Assign Roles and Responsibilities:  For larger teams, establish a clear hierarchy for managing community interactions.

Remember, community management is an ongoing process.  By fostering a welcoming and engaging environment, you cultivate brand loyalty, gain valuable customer insights, and turn your social media presence into a powerful marketing asset.

"Bonus Tip: Social media communities are living entities. Be prepared to adapt your approach based on audience feedback, emerging trends, and evolving platform features.

# Chapter-16

## Mastering Social Media Trends and Algorithms

The social media landscape is constantly evolving. New trends emerge, algorithms shift, and what worked yesterday might not be as effective today. This chapter module equips you with the knowledge and tools to stay up-to-date with the latest social media trends and algorithms, ensuring your social media strategy remains relevant and impactful.

### Why Stay Informed?

Staying ahead of the curve offers several advantages:

- Maximize Reach and Engagement: Leveraging trending topics and formats allows you to tap into a wider audience and generate higher engagement.
- Optimize Content Strategy: Understanding algorithm changes helps tailor your content to achieve better visibility and reach.
- Identify Emerging Opportunities: Spotting new trends allows you to be an early adopter and capitalize on emerging marketing opportunities.

## Strategies for Staying Informed

• Follow Social Media Platforms: Each platform has its own blog or newsroom where they announce updates and algorithm changes. Stay tuned for official announcements directly from the source.

• Industry News and Blogs: Subscribe to reputable social media marketing publications and blogs. These sources analyze algorithm changes, discuss emerging trends, and offer valuable insights.

• Social Media Marketing Forums & Groups: Join online communities dedicated to social media marketing. Engage in discussions, share knowledge, and stay updated on the latest industry buzz.

• Social Media Influencers: Follow thought leaders and influencers in the social media marketing space. They often discuss trends, analyze platform changes, and offer valuable perspectives.

• Podcasts: Listen to industry podcasts that cover social media marketing and discuss emerging trends. This allows you to stay informed while on the go.

• Competitor Analysis: Monitor your competitors' social media presence. See what content formats they use, which platforms they prioritize, and what kind of engagement they generate. Identify best practices and learn from their strategies.

• Social Media Analytics Tools: Leverage social media analytics tools that provide insights into trending topics and user behavior. Utilize these tools to identify relevant conversations and adapt your strategy accordingly.

**Tools and Resources**

Here are some helpful tools and resources to stay informed:

Social Media Platform Blogs:
- Facebook Newsroom
- Twitter Blog
- Twiends
- Instagram Newsroom
- Social Media Today
- Social Media Examiner
- Hootsuite Social Media Blog
- Reddit
- business.linkedin.

**Social Media Influencers:**

- Gary Vaynerchuk
- Neil Patel
- Seth Godin

**Social Media Marketing Podcast**

- podcasts.apple.

**Social Media Analytics Tools:**

- Brandwatch
- Buzzsumo
- Sprout Social

Remember: Staying informed is an ongoing process. Develop a routine for checking social media news, industry blogs, and competitor updates. By dedicating time to stay ahead of the curve, you'll be well-equipped to adapt your social media strategy and capitalize on the latest trends and algorithm changes.

## Conclusion

In this book, "How to Become a Social Media Manager with No Experience: Your Roadmap to Social Media Management," we have navigated through the essential steps and strategies to kickstart your career in social media management. From understanding the core responsibilities of a social media manager to mastering key tools and techniques, we've covered a comprehensive roadmap that demystifies the path to success in this dynamic field.

Starting without prior experience might seem daunting, but with dedication, continuous learning, and practical application of the insights shared here, you can build a solid foundation and grow into a proficient social media manager. Remember, the digital landscape is constantly evolving, and staying adaptable, curious, and proactive in honing your skills will keep you ahead of the curve.

Thank you for embarking on this journey with me through "How to Become a Social Media Manager with No Experience." I hope the guidance and tips provided in these pages inspire confidence and clarity as you take your first steps into the world of social media management. Your passion and perseverance are your greatest assets. Stay committed, keep experimenting, and never stop learning. The possibilities are endless, and your future as a social media manager is bright. Wishing you success and fulfillment in all your endeavors.

Sincerely,

M.I.Fazil